Organizing Yourself

Getting Organized with these Simple Strategies

Contents

Introduction

A good balance of your time is needed for work, goals, recreation, and relaxation. Being busy will keep your mind off worry because you will not be thinking of two different things at one time. The more organized you are the more time you will have for yourself. Read nonfiction books to increase your knowledge of everyday things in life and to learn new skills or to improve on existing ones. As you become better organized, take on a new after-hours project. This will give you a new purpose in life, a feeling of achievement and a good feeling of contentment. "It is simply a matter of noticing things and organizing them. You just have to care about what is around you and have a concern with humanity."

Set aside time for your own unique enjoyment. When you do this, staying organized will not feel as much of a chore. Being well organized takes lots of time and effort and there is a lot to remember. Ralph Waldo Emerson: "When I go into my garden with a spade, and dig a bed, I feel such an exhilaration and health". "I have been defrauding myself all this time in letting others do for me what I should have done with my own hands." Ralph Waldo. Emerson (1803-1882)

Have it in mind "Organized"

This involves a series of tips on how to stay organized. A keen memory is a well-nourished mind. Eat healthy; get plenty of rest and lots of good exercise will all see you through to having a good memory. Take advantage of alarm clocks and timers throughout your day. There are many good and free e-mail reminder services available for those who want to remember important events in the future. Use sticky notes to help jog your memory and call ahead to leave a message on your office answering machine to remember what you want to do when you are at work. If you keep saying you have a bad memory, you will probably continue to have a poor memory, says Dr. Rick McGahey.   Some chores are best left to only one pair of hands. You really do not want a second pair of meddling hands anyway. That way, you can

Get Rid of all clutter

Assign everything in your house a place. When your family searches for something they need, they will know exactly where to find it and where to put it away. When using stairs, never go up or down them empty-handed. Get rid of all junk drawers, or allow yourself just one that you clear out once a week or more. Hang hooks for your keys and purse at the entry to your home, so each time you walk in, you can hang them up. Establish one defined place in your home for storing library books, and end a house-wide hunt when it is time to read or return the books. Keep items that are used frequently in places where you can reach them without stooping or bending, and store them close to the place they will be needed. Take a moment to observe what things pile up and then come up with a new mantra: everything has its place and a place for everything. Take time to clear off the clutter of items left out "for now"

Organizing your home will free your mind to remember your daily chores. Getting rid of your clutter and organizing your home top to bottom is essential to staying on top of your chores. Be vigilant about cleaning about once a month and you will find it much easier to keep up, week-by-week.

Clutter is a Toll Order if left to prevail

Clutter and mess only serves to bring unbalance and will dampen any good spirit. Cleaning up and de-cluttering your kitchen will open space for you to receive the support and comfort that you need in life. Are you hiding yourself from others, by burying yourself in nasty clutter? You need clear hallways to navigate through your home. Your clutter in your hallways prevents important connections between different areas of your home and your life. Each day we use this important space to meet the world. We begin our days from this room. Clutter in the bathroom can mean you don't take pride in how you look and feel. Do you feel a disconnection between work and family, self and others, what you need to be done and your obligations? It may be time to give your hallway some good organizing. Do they contain good lighting and are they easily navigable, or do they cause confusion and trip you up? Are they important to you?

A well-decorated bathroom is a tranquil sanctuary for rejuvenation and self-care. Closets are everything hidden, unknown, or unrecognized. Clutter in the bedroom is worse than in any room. A cluttered attic causes you to feel under pressure. The basement and other below-ground storage areas are thought to be holders of the subconscious mind. Take the time to transform your bathroom into a place of refuge and this will bring a sense of the sacred into your morning and evening personal-care rituals, author says. You can beautify your life by organizing and cleaning this important room. Think of your car as a symbol of your agility, independence, and ability to be self-propelled in life.

De-cluttering

Paper clutter is a very good example. Loose paper can be found in every area of your home. Free yourself of clutter and open the flood gates of joy and energy into your life, author says. Having more time to spend your hours doing what you enjoy most is everyone's goal in life, he says. "Free yourself now of clutter," he says, and be prepared to move forward in your life as well. "Think of de-cluttering as one of the most effective self-improvement exercises available to you," author says. "Free yourself from clutter".

Organize your home by using a paper flow system. As soon as you receive the paper, you put it in its allotted place. The more time and effort you put into being organized, the less time you will need to apply to organizing later. Shop the discount and specialty stores for great tools to organize. There is no easy way around trying to get your life in order and be better organized. The moment you find the right tool; you can begin to put things into their proper place. Back to the page that you came to. The same system can be applied to reorganizing a disordered environment. Go from room to room in your home and apply tools to simplify messy problems.

Living an Orderly life

There are two types of people who exist in the work place: The Organized and The Disorganized. Getting proper instruction and a sense of guidance, the Disorganized can turn around on a dime and become organized. Find a way to peacefully get The Dis organized to change their ways and you will foster better habits. The Organized see to it that "everything has a place and that there's a place for everything" in the workplace. It is important to change adverse conditions in order to survive in harmony in the office. "The Organized" is a unique breed. They seem to be able to create handy places for things. They can generally get more done in a relatively short period. They have a real knack for tackling work with a disciplined approach. They are the ones you would call on first when you need help to get something important done.

Organized people thrive on having everything done in an orderly fashion. The minute The Disorganized becomes organized, the minute they have more time for themselves. Remember that whatever is not put in its place will only pile to make clutter. Even the most organized person can struggle with being orderly. We are often too busy to change our behavior. Developing a good routine takes time. The act of putting something away right away may sound easy for some, yet, on the other hand, is not part of some individual's basic nature. We are often too busy to make changes that we need to make in our daily lives to make a difference in the lives of those around us more orderly. It can be done if done carefully. It really only takes a moment but, if you do not, it can take hours to sort out when it gets out of control. It does not take long for every day mail to pile up if it is not being put away in his place as you finish with it. The best thing you can do for yourself now is change your attitude.

If you want to be clutter-free, have all of your projects in order. As you finish one, put it away before you begin on the next. Clear off your desk at the end of the day to make way for more work to come later. There is simplicity in order and organization, writes author Anne Morrow Lindbergh. "For the most part, we, who could choose simplicity, choose complication," she says. Anne Morrow Lindbergh, in *"Gift from the Sea"*, writes about getting rid of "stuff" in the home. "There is nothing more tiring than having to clear the way from the day before to start anew." Mrs. Lindberg, in her book,

"The Art of Tidying Up," says organizing is the key to a happy home and a happy life. She says it is important to make it a habit to work on just one project at a time and put away the unfinished work before moving on.

The more time you give yourself, the more you will get done, author says. Getting rid of stuff can be a real emotional undertaking for some people. Memories are usually attached to everything we own and, because of this, it can be difficult to let go. The best part of being organized is the amount of new space created, writer says. It's easy to get organized if you have a motivated, enthusiastic approach, he says. The author advises that even small bursts of time to get better organized can make a big difference.

Organization Art

You can get Organized too

There is a definite art to approaching the task of getting organized. Clutter interferes with your sense of tranquility and energy flow in your home. Objects actually have a frequency of energy, and clutter will interfere with the smooth flow of energy in any surrounding space. A room that has good order to it is a happy place to live and enjoy. We should all take pride in our home. Our home should be our refuge away from the storms in life, our home should also be our castle. The more organized your home, the more fun it will be to live in and enjoy it.

Design your kid's room so that they can keep it up themselves. Show your kids how to maintain their own rooms and reward them on their achievement. Give your kids their own household responsibilities and chores and then offer them a form of allowance. The more you sort through your personal belongings and find a new home for them, the more you'll find a home. Take the organizing plunge today. Do not put it off for one more moment in time. Your time is valuable to you. Use it wisely. A Few Good

Organizing Tips and Tricks. Have a work of art when you are done.

Have everything put in its assigned place, the area will be an

environment that smiles back at you when you enter it. You will be

proud! You will feel peace and joy. You'll be proud. It will make you

feel happy and relaxed. It'll make you happy. It's worth it. It just will

make your life feel better. It. Will make you happier and more

productive in the long run. More free space you will be opening up.

Determine your home style

Organizing your home is a matter of determining the style

you wish your home to have. A hassle-free lifestyle will not just

happen; you will make it happen. A system can be implemented on

anything, just as everything has a sort of "flow chart" to it. It is all

about how you manage your activity that makes the difference. If

you learn better time management, for instance, the result is more

time to do those chores you need to do. The more time you give to your family, the more you will have to spend on your home, so make sure you set aside time for them.

Every element of your life is affected by poor organization skills, says author. Clutter is one of the causes of not having time in the first place, he says. Visualize about what you want your area to look like to get an organized home. Creating an organized life at home works in the same fashion at your place of employment, he writes. Too many personal belongings placed everywhere around your home will not provide a sense of harmony. It is the harmony you are after and not the "things," he says, and it can be stressful and time-consuming to clean up after yourself. The author recommends decorating your home with photos from decorating magazines to get more organized in the spirit of your home and work space, and visualizing what you like best for your space.

When these elements are in place, it keeps stress levels lower for everyone in your family.

Organizing for a harmonic lifestyle at home requires that you put things in order that are meaningful to you and your family. Take up methodical and organized procedures that help you run your family like an organization. Involve other family members in sharing responsibilities. Engage everyone, in one facet or another. The harmony and peace will affect everything that you do. You will rest and play with new meaning and purpose. It may not happen overnight, but it will happen in time. It will be a pleasant place to visit, share, and make new friends. It can be a showcase of where you live your life with purpose and meaning. Others will take note and will want to come over and share your home with you. The more things that are in order, the more harmonious your home will be. It is a place where you feel like a million dollars. Do this and you will feel better about yourself. It won't happen overnight.

There are a number of organizational solutions to put into effect in the household. If there is a particular problem area, a system can be adapted to solve the problem. Create organized procedures and methods in your home and you will become organized. Have time on your side. We should all work very hard and when we do, we are bound to struggle through the pressures of life. We all have some unique problems in doing or achieving this aim. The first thing to realize is that you are not managing time too.

Well organized person

In order to manage yourself, establish your priorities. Deciding what you want to do is the first step to finding the time to do it. Life is more fulfilling when you are doing those things because they bring you joy. You do not need to sacrifice career, family, and wellbeing to achieve balance in your life. The way you view your activities has a great deal of impact on how you approach them, writes Mark Manson. You can opt to take any task and turn it into a purposeful one, giving it importance and meaning, he says. If you do it any other way, it is just a chore, Manson says. It is not something created for you, he writes. It's up to you. You have many different choices, he adds. You don't even need to change jobs either, just change your lifestyle. The choices you make have to do with doing things that align with your purpose or spirit, Manson writes. The more activities that bring joy to your life, the more fulfilled you will be.

Step off the "work speedway" even temporarily and regain a sense of balance. Separate what is important to you in your personal life. Develop a personal agenda that includes "your time" for family, friends, health, and passions. Allot various times of the day and week for certain activities.

Organize a Bit at a Time

Organize your junk drawer

It is easy to transform junk drawers into neatly organized compartments. The first big step to organizing a drawer is creating dividers. Use an egg carton for the little items that end up in a junk drawer. Film canisters can be used to collect small items such as change, tacks and buttons. A pre-assembled utility basket or even a utensil holder will help quickly get things in good order.

Clear out all of the clutter and remove everything but the machines and large furniture. Locate a good sorting area. If you do not have one, make one. Store your necessities in attractive canisters and decorative jars. Where you have extra space, place a wheeled cart between your machines for added storage. Voila! You have a new laundry room made to order! The ultimate laundry room makeover is a breeze, and it will save you time and money.

Disruptive kids are a form of disorganization in itself, taking time and energy from parents. Devise a system of effective control using earned rewards and praise. Teach your children to earn their place by being a contributing part of it. Be encouraging. Let them know there is always next time, and let them know they can do better, but do not sway in your position. It has to be as real as if they were going to a real job and being paid for their production. The rules agreed to have must be the rules.

Organize your garage

Many American homeowners live with a landfill attached to their homes. Start by having a garage sale, give to charity, take a trip to the real landfill, and take a deep breath. Get rid of all the excess that not only blocks entry into the home but the clutter that blocks energy too. One of the easiest methods is to create a wall storage solution such a hooks, racks, custom-made cabinets, and yes, the lowly nail is a solution, but none offer a flexible solution. Drill drywall screws into the grooves of the panels into the studywall in the garage and then install. Hooks fit in the groove nicely, making placement a snap. The hooks are manufactured in varying lengths from one inch to 12 inches, so a variety of objects can be placed anywhere there is a wall. The product needs no painting or maintenance. Made with a durable finish, it needs no maintenance. It is made in 4' x 8' panels, and these same grooved panels offer the most flexible storage solution for the garage.

Look, flexibility and durability are all superior benefits from Displawallä. Rubbermaid cabinets are both affordable and durable. There is nothing to paint and nothing to maintain. All that you need is a rubber mallet to hammer the interlocking pieces together. Load capacity is about 35 pounds according to the manufacturer. There are no holes to drill or nails to hammer simply arrange or rearrange the hooks, as you desire. The concepts outlined above are very basic and you will personalize as it best meets with your particular need. It is a good start to being better organized and you can work through the glitches as they happen. It takes time and effort. All it takes is good ingenuity and good planning. You will reap the rewards each day!

Organize your child's study habits

How a study "headquarters" is set up affects a child's ability to stay focused. Establish school supply storage solutions to organize various school materials. Set up a disciplined homework routine. Use tools to motivate and encourage learning. If you can afford to, get a computer. Research has shown that children who master computers will learn faster.

To help with your child's studying habits, try these eight tips.

If you have young children, create an award chart to give kids some incentive to do their schoolwork, by rewarding them for completing assignments.

Set up a daily schedule. Establish daily schedule forms to delegate

the amount of time needed for the most important study priorities.

Set up a study group to improve one's studies. Take good notes.

Outlining a textbook or article helps distinguish the most important

facts and points. A horizontal or vertical timeline will help visualize

the chronology. Build a concept tree to help make notes more

memorable and present a visual representation of the relationship

among several essential facts. Design a note card system to cut

down the time it takes to research and organize your term paper.

Organize your kitchen

Use the cupboards and drawers in the kitchen to contain

items that are grouped together. Food should be gathered with like-

items together, and not spread out into different cabinets. Get away

from cluttering the counters with too many appliances. Establish a

place in your kitchen to keep a message center and/or paper-related

items, like a note pad and pens near the phone. It's a good idea to clean out the refrigerator weekly to be rid of foods that have "expired" and smell up your fridge. The kitchen is the heart of the home and is a gathering place, a special place. It is the most memorable place to make your home a home -- and your kitchen is a perfect spot for a party.

Put the Word "Organized" Back into your Life!

Organizing yourself is the KEY if you want to have time to do the things you enjoy. Use a day planner to lay out your day so you know where you are going and what you are doing. Buying a family planner will let you know what everyone in the family is up to and when. Exercise your stress management techniques by saying "no" occasionally when you are asked to do things that are of little priority to you. Take time to enjoy yourself. What makes you the happiest? Spending time with your children? Going out to the movies? Indulging at the spa? Attending sports or shows? Take a minute to think of what you love to do most and then get out there and do it all!

When was the last time you organized that junk drawer, or sorted through your fridge? Chances are, you might be spending valuable time getting frustrated over missing items. Establish a good routine. Keep writing in your planner daily and keep scheduling time for yourself. Stick with your new routine and you will find you will be happier and with much less stress. The number one benefit to being better organized is being sane!

Ways to get organized

Being a list person is a great help. There are clever ways to help organize your life and keep your sanity. Establish a time limit for each telephone call and make sure you tell your caller. Do not allow for the luxury of procrastination. If you do, this will only stress you out when you think about that hateful "to do" item on your list. You will end up stressed out and with no time to do anything. The next time someone helps you out with something, be sure to offer praise. They will be happy to help you again, next time you need them. We all search for good ways to organize our lives, but here are a few tips to help us get the most out of our lives.

We are a team of super-busy people who want to make the world a better place.

Start by tackling the largest or most disliked job first, dividing it up into manageable tasks. Delegate those tasks that you have no time for or team up with someone who can help you most. Go through your entire file system and then weed out any old unneeded files to free up space in your filing system. Use those handy sticky notes to write errands needed to be done. Find a new system that works for you and your lifestyle and then apply it to absolutely everything. You simply find there is too much time wasted every day on searching for things. Find your own systems engineer. Find new time slots you never thought existed. Use it like clockwork and you will find new time slot you. Never thought existed! You will find it like clockwork and it will work for you!

C.O.P.E

When it comes to balancing a family, including young children, a home and perhaps a career, you have choices. The secret to success in organizing is the ability to prioritize your various commitments, enlist the help of others.

Capitalize

Do more with your children and less for your children. Train them very early to put away their toys and make their own beds. Put all of your perfectionist tendencies aside while your kids are growing up.

Organize

Organize your home to make it easier to locate and store things. Large shelves or a huge toy chest and hangers placed where children can reach them are good examples.

Prioritize

You cannot do everything but you can do lots. Pick the most important activity and then concentrate on getting it done. Do what is really important, not simply the things that need to be done.

Energize

Energize yourself by getting plenty of rest, eat all of the right foods and adhere to an exercise program. Being physically fit and mentally alert will allow you to handle those stressful situations.

Organize your move

Moving can be traumatic or it can be a new adventure for the whole family. Some items you will keep, some you will give away and lots you will trash. Keep the stuff someone else will find usable so give to charity as you leave. This will make unpacking much easier once you arrive. Keep your linen closet items together. Keep bathroom items together, tools or garage items in as many boxes as is necessary. It is that simple! It can all be a very uplifting experience, honest it can! Now, start packing by area.

Establish an organized office

Use these organizing tips to have a professional and efficient home office. Send regular follow-ups, reminders, and communications to clients. Prepare and send invoices to clients and enter monthly transactions into bookkeeping software. Maintain a newsletter subscription database. Post announcements and newsletter issues to the list. Edit or upload new information to a website. Follow these tips to help you organize your home office and market your products. The Daily Discussion is a weekly, offbeat look at what's going on in the office. The Daily Discussion includes tips on how to organize your office and make the most of your time. At the bottom of the page, share your organizing tips for a well-organized home office with your friends and family. Find out which locations have the appropriate dates available for an event and which can accommodate the size and type of event. Store back-up computer tapes for safekeeping. Track birthdays, anniversaries, and other important dates. Send out the appropriate cards or gifts for special events. Manage lists of necessary office supplies and ordering refills. Coordinate air travel, car rental, and hotel reservations. Check spelling / grammar for spelling and grammar errors in documents. Keep paper that requires an action on your part stored separately from items that you are keeping just for reference purposes. Try to keep paper that needs to be done by you separate from items you keep just for your reference purposes, such as pens and pencils.

Use "L" and "U" shaped desks for the most efficient workspaces. Store gadgets and equipment on one "wing" and leave the other free to spread out while you work. Pay special attention to your body - aches and pains aren't normal. Do not generally bend, squat, or stretch at your workstation. Use a separate supply area for storing bulk amounts and store paper, notepads, clips, and folders in stacking trays. Use bracket shelves above your desk for additional storage and file away extra items in drawers and labeled containers.

Hire an organizer

Professional Organizers serve as holistic "clutter doctors" to free up the soul. Eradicate the cause of disorganization, as well its symptoms and you will be free. Set up proven, effective, easy-to-use organizing systems to de-clutter the mind. Reduce all forms of clutter (Get rid of anything that wastes time, space, energy, or money) Create systems that make everyday jobs easier (Develop effective routines and standardized procedures) Simplify daily responsibilities (Reduce the amount of time and energy spent on routine activities). They monitor and encourage your ongoing progress (Offer follow-up visits, phone calls, coaching, and "homework" assignments). They teach organizing techniques -- also keep clients motivated and focused. They wear many hats -- educator, resource, coach, and cheerleader, project manager. They help change behaviors that cause disorganization (Procrastinating, failing to plan ahead, and accumulating "excess stuff").

Take Control of Chronic Disorganization

Jerri felt trapped by the contents of her home and desperate to change a situation that was paralyzing her life. Jerri confessed that she had always found it impossible to be organized. "It's overwhelming. I just don't want to live like this anymore," she said.

"Daily life should not be so hard!" is the mantra most commonly uttered by those who feel overwhelmed by the chaos in their homes, she says. "Chaos and clutter is a circle, a maddening one! For some people, this is an occasional scenario, but for others, the constant confusion disables an otherwise productive life," she says. The author is the wife and mother of two young children, who live in a home in New York City with her husband and three children. The book is based on a TED Talk series "Tired of Clutter," hosted bycom/Heroes of the Co-Stars. "Being organized" is not a goal worthy of your investment for its own sake, but "being organized" can make other goals manageable. You could hire a professional organizer and pick their brains for tips and hints that you could acquire all on your own. Accumulating mess, junk and clutter can reach huge proportions for some. Jerri went with the professional coach. She knows that the time they spend together will be both fun and freeing. In addition, best of all, today, sunlight fills Jerri's home. The coach has taught her to look for the gems amidst the garbage and mess and that includes a gem of an idea. It's a treasure hunt.

The gem is an idea, and Jerri has a new strategy for moving beyond

her disorganization.

Organizing yourself if you are a busy mom

Time cannot be managed but people can, writes author. Instead of managing it, we must manage ourselves and use our time well, he says. Establish priorities. Decide whether you want to be the Chief, Cook and Bottle washer or the MANAGER. The way to claim more time for yourself is to become a great manager and train others in your household to do more of the work in your place, he writes. The hardest part is to be brave, says author, and be willing to try something new and try something different. "Be brave. Be a manager. Be the best you can be," writes author, who lives in the U.S. with his wife and three children in New Jersey. "That's where the time is at. It's the only time you have for yourself," he says, "so go for it!" Set a timer when doing certain activities to keep track of just how much time you are putting into any activity. Shop with a list or even a timer. Do your errands when the stores are the least busy. Avoid shopping on the busiest days and the busiest times. Group tasks by type and location to speed up your daily chores. "Shopping as a chore and not a hobby" is a good way to save time in the shop. It will save you time and money in the long run and reduce the amount of time you lose by doing what you need to do.

Always plan ahead for what you will need. Leave free time in your day for when life is unpredictable. Stop saying yes to every club, PTA, and acquaintance that asks you to do something. As soon as your children are old enough, teach them how to take care of organizing, cleaning, and other household maintenance. Teach your spouse as well. This will blend harmony into the fabric of your lives and give you more time for yourself and your family.

Final home organizing. Where to start

Organization is not an option, it is a fundamental survival skill and distinct competitive advantage. Start anywhere in your home, but with just one problem area. Choose an organizational system that you know you will be able to work with easiest. Decide on a suitable place for items you have accumulated over the years, which are waiting to be sorted, filed or acted on. If paper management (or whatever area you are trying to improve) is easy for you, you would not be in this bind in the first place. Do not try to do all your organizing first, before implementing your new system. Simply gather your collection of papers, deposit them in a designated place, and work on them. It's easier than trying to organize a house that's not organized, says Pam N. Woods, author of Organize Your Home.

 Start using your system immediately. 10 or 15 minutes per day will work down the pile in no time. If you find that the system you are using does not address a particular need, make a decision about this straight away. You can change your system at any point and reorganize things, so do not wait for the perfect idea before you try something new. Use the system like clockwork. That is the only way any system will work well for you.

The advantages of organization

You'll sense yourself better.

You're going to feel more relaxed.

Your world's going to smell and look sweeter.

You're going to be politer.

Family and friends are going to want to go in.

A brighter smile is going to wear your spouse and baby.

You're going to have happy dreams.

You're not going to slip at home.

More compliments would be paid by citizens.

Your kitchen's going to smell more scented.

Your soul could better breath.